THE NEXT BLUE NOTE

JOE NEAL

Copyright © Joe Neal 2017

All rights reserved. No part of this publication may be reproduced or transmitted in any form or by any means, electronic or mechanical including photocopying, recording or any information storage or retrieval system, without prior permission in writing from the publishers.

The right of Joe Neal to be identified as the author of this work has been asserted by him in accordance with the Copyright, Designs and Patents Act 1988

First published in the United Kingdom in 2017 by
The Choir Press

ISBN 978-1-911589-07-5

Printed in size 11 Cambria.
Edited by Harriet Evans.
Portrait of the author by Tommy Clancy.
Cover design by Jacqueline Abromeit.

ALSO BY JOE NEAL

Telling It at a Slant, Pen Press (2013).
ISBN 978 1 78003 664 9

Turn Now the Tide, Choir Press (2014).
ISBN 978 1 909300 73 6

Hear the Colour, Choir Press (2015).
ISBN 978 1 910864 13 5

Still Rise the Sun, Choir Press (2016).
ISBN 978 1 910864 61 6

Readings by the author from these poetry collections can be heard at:

www.joenealtellingitataslant.com
www.turnnowthetide.com
www.hearthecolour.com
www.stillrisethesun.com

ABOUT THE AUTHOR

Joe Neal was born half-way up a mountain in North Wales. He began his acting career in repertory theatre before attending Nottingham University. He also trained as a journalist, working for the Western Mail (Cardiff), Times, Guardian, Daily Telegraph and Daily Express.

As an actor, he has performed on stage, radio and television in Britain and Ireland. Between acting work Neal writes extensively on the countryside and natural history as well as devoting time to poetry and short stories which he believes should be read aloud – 'even to oneself.'

He writes of life and all its strife and tells it at a slant – sometimes with the delight of a child rolling boulders down a slope. His poems plunder dreams and memories and bend to the natural world. He says, 'Love, I'm afraid, is a constant theme: lost loves, found loves, hoped-for loves, hopeless love. Mostly the last. But as Clint Eastwood says in the character of Dirty Harry, "A man's got to know his limitations."'

A glutton for punishing experiences, he stood twice as an Independent for Parliament in Britain and once in Ireland for the European elections.

His published work has appeared in the Times, Daily Telegraph, Countryman, Waterlog, New Writer, New Society (now defunct), Ireland's Own, Scaldy Detail and numerous poetry magazines. Performed writing includes *Revenge*, *The Reluctant Trombonist*, *Send in the Clown* and *Kites and Catullus*. He has read the poems of

Seamus Heaney and John Betjeman on BBC television and Shakespeare and Dylan Thomas on BBC radio. Recently he had 12 of his poems published in the anthology *Dust Motes Dancing in the Sunbeams*.

The Next Blue Note is Neal's fifth collection of poetry and follows the widely acclaimed *Still Rise the Sun* (2016), *Hear the Colour* (2015), *Turn Now the Tide* (2014) and *Telling It at a Slant* (2013). All are available through major book stores worldwide and on Amazon. The author has recorded his readings of all five publications.

Neal says his life has been shaped by his childhood in Morfa Bychan, Gwynedd, North Wales and the Roman town of Colchester, Essex, and – more importantly – by time spent in Ireland, where he now lives. He is divorced and a proud grandparent.

*Love is an albatross
– but don't shoot it!*

CONTENTS

Foreword	i
CAMBODIAN SMILE	
Cover Girl	1
Cambodian Smile	2
Songs for Swingeing Lovers	3
Those Were the Days	4
Moontrap	5
Release	6
The Day We Went to Nantmor	7
For the Birds	8
Star You Are	9
Boundless Night	10
Innocence	11
And Now I Do Without	12
Haiku Too Far	14
Bye-Bye Blues	15
A Word in Your Ear	16
Box Linnet	17
Breath of Bechet	18
Train Robber	20
Last Flower	21
Ragtime Cowboy	22
Mountain Slide	24

Belfast Boom	25
The Books That Fell on Me	26
Fishing	28
Not What It Seems	29
Boating Bonhomie	30
Degaussing	32
Long-Tailed Tit	33
Make Believe	34
Standing Room Only	35
Knowingly	36
Funny Valentine	37
Water	38

LADY BE BETTER

Moon	41
Trumpet Smile	42
Turn and Turnabout	44
Jazz Me Blues	45
Fame Game	46
Tidal Race	47
Bog Beginnings	48
You Again!	49
Off-Beat	50
Moving On	51
No Sting in the Tale	52
Absolutely	53
Cave Paintings	54
Wilderness	56

Cool for Cats	57
On Reflection	58
Hey-Ho!	59
Alien	60
Buried Treasure	61
Test of Time	62
An Evening with Courtney Pine	63
Ill Met by Sunlight	64
Lady Be Better	66
Nuts!	67
By the Seaside	68
Slice of Life	70
Weather Warning	71
Passing	72

ALLEGHENY MAN

Mountain Greenery	75
On State Street	76
Go with the Flow	78
I Had a Dream	79
Allegheny Man	80
Night Life	82
Shake and Rattle	84
Crossed Lines	85
Like Father, Like Son	86
What to Do	88
Lean of Life	89
Again	90

Condition Red	91
All Dressed in Black	92
Horses for Courses	93
Good Morning Blues	94
Pity the Wind	95
Holey Moley!	96
The Hare That Dipped Its Paws	97
Time Change	98
Seeing Is Believing	99
Inside Out	100
Blueing the Blues	101
Moments	102
Card-Bored	103
Sounds Familiar	104
Trouble Ahead?	106
Swimming with a Manatee	107
Deep Blue Sea	108
Sorrel	109

FOREWORD

*And now I do without
the stinging clout
of love –
the heft that humps the hurt
that least expects
attack.*

(from 'And Now I Do Without')

Our world changed significantly during the gestation of the many poems which make up the foundation of *The Next Blue Note*, Joe Neal's fifth collection in as many years.

Yet somehow, in spite of the uncertainties of Brexit and the Trump administration, Neal continues to hew original jewels of verse, insulated from the machinations of the outside world.

*... around the Mull and setting sun
inflames the separating sea between;
stars wink down lovingly – bounded island
yet still boundaried, united now by night.
A heron beats a path from north to south.*

(from 'Boundless Night')

Neal's world is a combination of the alluvia of memory deposited by interchangeable time, and the joie de vivre of the natural world which is the palpable beat of Eden Vale, outside Wexford, where he lives, and where he observes the flora and the fauna, and where he writes, and writes. Later in the summer when the sea trout explore the River Sow and carry the light of the moon on their backs, Neal will consider the prospect of casting a dry fly, and in this ritualistic experience, a poem is born. The essence of the experience is the poet's hunger and willingness to connect.

I see Neal as a Welsh-Wexford version of Thoreau's Walden, and many of his poems are an experiment in day-to-day living, in observation and, naturally, in what it means to love and to lose and to love again and to lose again. The ongoing cycle, part and parcel of the poet's circadian rhythm, is the fodder of a curious and sensitive mind. Like Thoreau, Neal remains enthralled by his intimacy with the animals and birds he comes into contact with, the smell and the sound of Eden Vale, the harsh and often cruel realities of seasonal changes: what emerges from his palette is a style both elegant and straightforward. But to his ear, there is always music in the wind.

I think the poems remind Neal that he is fulfilling an almost primeval desire to live as simply and as self-sufficiently as possible, as anybody who has tried to communicate with him by text or e-mail can vouch.

Readers of Neal's poems who are familiar with *Hear the Colour*, *Telling It at a Slant*, *Still Rise the Sun* and *Turn Now the Tide* will acknowledge his keen faculties for the mood in the sound of a line, the ambience conveyed in a simple brushstroke of words, and how a poem can toll out by whispering softly.

A big coin moon shines on me tonight,
the kind that wishes for a face,
smiling at my fecklessness
as I try to find a missing word
to complete this jigsaw life.

(from 'Moon')

Coursing through the poems in this collection, I sense that an approach by the poet which segues *The Next Blue Note* with the previous books is threefold, mirroring (but not necessarily deliberately) the early Romantics. First, Neal displays in his work the sense of a new and reinvigorating attitude to nature. Second, the poet is unafraid to use poetry as a tool to comprehend his own psychology, digging deeply into his sensibility and perception and, third, expressing his faith in his work to be at the centre of his experience and, in a sense, in the great tradition of early nineteenth-century rural English poetry, the first and last of all knowledge. Neal places great emphasis on feeling, instinctively and intuitively: it is not rehearsed, but the intensity is never the poorer for that, and in return he can unleash lyrics that are like great fluorescent stealth bombers: '*The nightjar swoops and yaws/and churrs its song, cracks/its white-blobbed wings/in little echoes off the* clog/*that rears from moorland heath*' (from 'Night Life').

How the world works and how the poet engages with it, dipping into the collective unconscious for archetypes to interpret and understand the intensity of his perceptions – be it jazz or love or lust or passion or incredulity in the face of God-like nature – is akin to

Shelley's nightingale who sings to cheer his own solitude.

In 'I Had a Dream', he asks, '*Do you ever get a feeling/that a place, a people past,/peels off on you? I do./ Sometimes it's as if/I get sucked in by the essence/of awareness and carry it/away with me when I move on.*' Neal's collections of poetry are as fluid as a stream, and I believe his trademark is how he weaves seamlessly, so there is an amorphousness between the worlds of love, of memory, of nature and of music. It is important to appreciate how much Neal views the imagination as the embodiment of human desire, without which his world could not exist. And with that sensibility comes passion, without which Neal's interest would flag. What Seamus Heaney said of Theodore Roethke, that he was outside movements and generations, and his work is a true growth, applies equally to Joe Neal.

> *... steep above them all,*
> *a kestrel hovers*
> *with the same intent;*
> *higher still, a silver streak*
> *tears a crevice in the sky.*
>
> *Night descends ...*

(from 'Night Life')

Tom Mooney
April 2017

Tom Mooney is executive editor of Ireland's Echo Group of Newspapers, an award-winning author and editor of the poetry anthology Dust Motes Dancing in the Sunbeams.

CAMBODIAN SMILE

Cambodian Smile

COVER GIRL

She waits on days to come
– blaze of modesty,
tilt of head
to hide the fear
that plunders bounds
of possibility
for one so young;
ask her how to do
the Charleston,
she'll shimmy off
a step or two
and glide across the floor
but has no sense of time
as Roaring Twenties
dawn and music mocks
a second war
just around the corner.

CAMBODIAN SMILE

Dawn light elongates the sky,
stretching pink like fingers
of a Cambodian smile –
Rodin reeling from the canvas
in swizzle-dance of line
that stirs the world to life again.

I remember this so well
because you were there to share
the moment when we woke,
reaching out to hold it
in the window frame of time,
laughing at our nakedness.

But now that you have gone,
the bluster-clouds that Turner
drew so dauntingly blot out
the bright – and grim the day
as I try to wrench you
from my mocking memory.

Cambodian Smile

SONGS FOR SWINGEING LOVERS

We play our favourite tunes
for ammunition now –
each time we have a row,
anger better said
in records than in words;

I strike first – Snake Rag
hissing from an old LP
bought at university
(not to beat adversity)
and cornets hit the high notes;

Shania Twain shouts back
in song, CD now takes aim
and misses with affection;
I'm Gonna Getcha Good!
she plays at me

without listening
to the words; we make up
with Psycho Killer
and embrace
the way we are.

The Next Blue Note

THOSE WERE THE DAYS

Those Were the Days, my friend:
it is a song for everyone,
tribute to the age we loved best,
and Mary Hopkin called it
for us all – how in our hearts
the dreams are still the same.

MOONTRAP

Gleam draws me to Tumble Mount
where a drizzle moon is caged
by careless trunks of trees –
and twilight owl soft-comforts
me with rhythm of its call.

Passing through the living bars,
I join the bright the other side
and watch stretched white wings
slide away like a dipping,
disappointed children's kite.

Bared now to interviewing
light, shouting thoughts are locked
into my head – until
a passing cloud unshackles me
and I dandy down the hill.

Darkness re-envelops me.

RELEASE

Finger twitch on fisted rein
sends a signal to the brain
of forward-reaching horse,
anticipating moment
of release from clip-clop gait
– and then she's off, beating back
the ground, daring nuzzled air
to hold her down again.

I think I know that moment now
– it was in the song we sang
together at the end,
blending bleeding hearts in such
a way that we found freedom
from each one – without descent
to music of a minor key
or words that had us hanging on.

And now we meet once more
to trot along a road the same
– and wonder who will break
the rhythm, so sedate,
we choose to hide the will
to make that great escape
from constraining ways that lull
our urge to nudge the air.

Cambodian Smile

THE DAY WE WENT TO NANTMOR[1]

Recalcitrant sun defies the wet air
with arches of colour laundered by rain,
again and again, until all comes out blue
and the sky looks the same as before.

Now with billy-can hiss and the prospect
of tea we ignore our damp clothes and chew
on a sandwich the Welsh mountain way:
picnicking weather on moist summer day.

---

[1] Nantmor, N. Wales. Rainfall 86in. Caves give shelter to hikers
– and lesser horseshoe bats.

FOR THE BIRDS

Quaint notions fall from you
like small heirlooms,
superstitious conjurings
of local memory;

You talk of mourning doves
and night-call owls,
two crows flying to the left
or tits pecking at the pane;

And if I should be taken first
you'll say you saw a hen
that crossed my path
to join me on the other side.

STAR YOU ARE

Turn now the syntax
just like Yoda speaks,
reversing words galactically:
slim volumes
star the wars of poetry.

The Next Blue Note

BOUNDLESS NIGHT

Eventime in Ireland's county Wexford,
the purple air inherits heat
from cooling sun-warmed earth below
and lustrous swan-flaked Slaney crawls
longingly along its well-cut course.

A diagonal away, Leitrim lights
its window to the waves and southpaw Kerry
punches at the ocean in Dingle jab
defensively; elsewhere, the Kintyre stare
of Antrim's Cushendun spreads a blush

around the Mull and setting sun
inflames the separating sea between;
stars wink down lovingly – bounded island
yet still boundaried, united now by night.
A heron beats a path from north to south.

Cambodian Smile

INNOCENCE

Uncluttered, blissful, ignorant of sin
– believing everything and nothing,
expecting something else from me,
I dare, as boy, to take your hand dangling,
our fingers touch along their length uncurled;
you smile, I look at you, seriously,
and you clutch at me with great intent;
a serpent's tongue licks around an apple.

The Next Blue Note

AND NOW I DO WITHOUT

And now I do without
the stinging clout
of love –
the heft that humps the hurt
that least expects
attack;

Drawbridge up, portcullis down,
impregnable
at last
to glance and siren voice
that bids me change
my ways;

Words brandy-whipped to floss,
converting mine
by your
extravagance to spade
stuck smotherings
of clay;

All the while I tremble-lip
my love in fear
of loss
before entrenchment makes
me old and cheats
my time;

Cambodian Smile

No more of this, I'll grow
immune to your
disdain,
for wisdom builds in me
the strength to wear
my plight;

Love is for everyone
– not just the two
to share
exclusively in want
of world around
aware.

The Next Blue Note

HAIKU TOO FAR

We met in some far-off bar,
a glance and double-take;
her eastern grace said *haiku*
and I configured clever
dialogue while ceremonies
of tea came to mind – she seemed
that kind of girl, serene
like snow-capped mountain or gentle

waves beneath a clenched-up sky;
and when I spoke, she said,
'You sound like a poet.
I feel uncomfortable
with that.' I gulped down the verse
and took my leave before
my napkin origami
made her really mad at me.

Cambodian Smile

BYE-BYE BLUES

This is music
of what might be
– your voice cajoling me,
caught breath
and then a shout,
laughing unselfconsciously
as we spank the sand
with sock-freed feet
and race towards the sea.

You lash the waves
and gasp
at their ice caress
while our legs
are lightened
by the undertow.

But this is as far
as I can get
as I try to conjure you,
watching that slide
towards the curtain,
grateful that the image
still splashes on my mind.
Brothers we, parted
so unexpectedly.

The Next Blue Note

A WORD IN YOUR EAR

Now 'worple' is a word
to conjure with.
Waking up with this in mind,
I tell it you – who repeats
it back, quizzically.
'Worple', what's that?
You know, I say, 'worple',
it can only mean one thing.
'Tush,' says you
– and we're exchanging
words again. Which can't be bad.
That's a start at least!

Cambodian Smile

BOX LINNET

Better you had ripped my wings
than locked me in this cage,
plucked out my eyes
so I'd never see the light again
– I'd sing the brighter
then in memory of the time
I once flew free.

BREATH OF BECHET

*– listening at home to Sidney Bechet's soprano
saxophone while the wind plays out a storm.*

Leaves that fall before their time,
like beech upended by a storm
and mourned as much by nature
as by man in whispered gather
of the light expanding,
while howl of wind in spaces left
changes frequency until
new growth comes to fill the gaps:

I think of this while listening
to the cadence of the notes
you blew in skitter-scatter
testament to grief and love
and downright sauciness –
trills and thrills of saxophone
describing reds and yellows,
greens and that inevitable blue;

Adulterous quavers queuing up
to crawl across the crotchets,
spanking out extended screech
of mournful semibreve, turning day
into a contradictory

Cambodian Smile

night of passionate embrace;
in another time my mood
may see it differently!

But when you blew you must have thought
of places where you'd been
and people met or seen in streets
you walked or pictured in a dream
– not of nature's storms like me,
bounded by my own perceptions
in a life so far removed
from jazzy jocularities.

Petite Fleur bleeds from Bechet's sax
as storm outside runs short of breath.

The Next Blue Note

TRAIN ROBBER

I remember Buster Edwards
for the dowdy plush of peonies
he gave away to me,
last blooms of a fading day –
one pair of damp chrysanths
thrown in to please;
'She'll like these,' he said,
after seeing us arguing.
He knew all his customers,
the Great Train Robber
selling flowers
to Charing Cross commuters
in penance for his sin.

Cambodian Smile

LAST FLOWER

If I dream
I pick a flower
and when I wake
I'm holding it
you'll know
I am no more.

The Next Blue Note

RAGTIME COWBOY

Pract-is-ing trombone,
I draw an audience
of sixty cows, munching
mournful as they eyeball
me in black and white despair;

Brown Eyes Why Are You
So Blue? I play to them,
blowing against the wind
as Autumn Leaves
swirl around my head;

But Hall of the Mountain King
stampedes them into stomp
as Ellington's Morning Song
powers along, *prestissimo*,
in piston-pumping jounce of slide;

It is my Ukelele Lady
that brings them
flouncing back again
– Black Bottom swaying
the Swipsy Cakewalk way;

Mooch and My Very Good Friend
the Milkman hold them close to me

Cambodian Smile

– until two bulls appear
with eyes that Blaze Away,
matching voltage of restraining wire;

Growling now, *rallentando*, I back off,
performance in the tailgate
mode, Dippermouth no match
for Bullhorn Rag – time
to beat retreat with Bye Bye Blues.

Pianissimo.

The Next Blue Note

MOUNTAIN SLIDE

He climbed fast,
black trombone case
strapped to his back
– Chicago gangster
out of place –
until he reached
the highest pitch,
mountain peak
at two thousand feet;
then, with slide at five,
he blew B-flat beat
with nothing there
to startle
with his blare
– 'cept an avalanche
of summer snow.

BELFAST BOOM

Upbraided from the corner
of his mouth, words peeling
out of funnel-curl of lips:
morning salutations
always sound so like a curse,
kindest thoughts delivered
with aggression – snarl the scar
of faction wars that make up
a noisy neighbourhood:
'Sun is mortal warm today!'
then, with universal grin:
'Brass monkey days are best for me.'

THE BOOKS THAT FELL ON ME

Sitting stocious on the floor,
I start to turn the pages
of the books that fell on me
when I embraced the shelves
in drunken search
of stimulating company.

First up, words whizzing round my head,
is *Avalanche Awareness*
by instructor Martin Epp
with whom I skied
off-piste from Andermatt
to Zermatt in a week.

It is full of bold advice:
'Like a bottle, roll your way
from out the snow sideways.'
This I do, probing as I go
to find other books
piled at foot of kitchen wall.

Jazz by Humphrey Lyttleton
has this to say to me:
'Blow your riff from memory.'
Words are floating now,
cascades of black and white
blueing music through the night.

Cambodian Smile

Seamus Heaney's squat pen writes
to me, *Death of a Naturalist*
pinning down my *British Birds*
and *Fishes of the Mountain
Lakes* – and Holy Bible shalt-nots
ringing in my ears, reading

taste all very catholic
(but not to blame it
on the pub alone);
now I shift my weight
and a last book falls
– *Under Milk Wood* – on my head.

FISHING

Hunched and rumpled man
stooping by the weir dam,
questioning the water
with sharpness of his hooks;

Brightly-coloured tip of quill
exclaims the presence of a fish
and leaning languor of his jutting rod
trembles into dipping jerk;

Far down below the river's
ruffled skin a pike swims past,
knowingly, and shoaling
tiddlers nudge the dangled

bait, sending little tremors
to the watching angler's float;
commanded from his reverie,
he strikes and sets the hook.

Cambodian Smile

NOT WHAT IT SEEMS

I met her on a miming course
and I think I fell in love
– at least that's how she made it seem
each time she looked at me;

Those wide blue eyes that fluttered
endlessly and trickled out
a tear she dabbed so gracefully
– before she put her lenses in;

My sad clown face was no pretence.
Years on, we met once more,
on stage to share a song –
and eyes flicked right, remembering.

BOATING BONHOMIE

Breezing into Isle of Bute
we sailed between two winds
– Mistral and Sirocco –
and snuggled up to Tasman,
Ginger Tom and Cherokee,
then scrambled up the quay
to make landfall at the pub.
Over plates of Loch Fyne prawns
and pints of heavy beer
we talked of submarines
we'd seen surfacing –
tossing us like flotsam,

halyards clacking as we slewed
about the curdled Clyde.
But all was well and missiles
stayed unlaunched as sailors waved
at us apologetically;
we laughed at this and gobbled
up some creamy Atholl brose
before re-joining sailing
sisters in slip-slap swell of loch.
Screech of fenders rubbing shoulders
with our neighbours kept us
constantly awake – until

Cambodian Smile

a squirt of Sqezy made sleep
easy as tall masts tilted
at the moon, knitting needles
crossing in the ripple sway.
Boating bonhomie on morning
tide saw us saying farewell
to Cherokee and Tasman,
Mistral and Sirocco
before we parted company
with Ginger Tom and headed
out of porridge-lumpy Rothesay
Sound in search of friends anew.

DEGAUSSING

Degaussing ships and submarines,
re-aligning north and south
to repel magnetic mines
lurking with the enemy;

Now we're in the loop,
electric fields are changing
– no longer poles apart,
like attracts us;

We are not just opposites,
you and me are one –
make love not war,
our life has just begun.

Cambodian Smile

LONG-TAILED TIT

In my jumble thicket
of a hedge – blackthorn,
bramble, mint and bay –
I spied a ball of moss
and spider web with feathers
sticking out and knew
a long-tailed tit had come
to build its nest with me.

A stick on frame of quarter ounce,
tiniest of that family,
with subtle pink of rump
that puts in mind the blush
of daunting Mrs Dalloway
as she descends the stairs.
Tzee-tzee-tzee, it sings
as it binds the dome in place.

But watching all the while,
another bird of black and white
with elongated tail;
the scene is set for tragedy
as magpie swoops and leaves
a curling feather cloud
to filter down through
blood-stained mint and bay.

MAKE BELIEVE

How does licked finger
tell the wind?
Or extended thumb
and digit five
take a call from you?

It's all make-believe,
mime too far-removed
from our reality;
a proper wind will lash
your hair and shout

from me will catch your ear
and bring a smile from you;
so do it, say it
as it is – oh, for goodness'
sake, let's just have a beer!

STANDING ROOM ONLY

Night-sleeping horses, ghostly
in the mist, upright, legs
floating out of sight, sleek heads
glistening in the moonlight
– I remembered then how *I'd* slept
standing once, my bed a red
phone box, locked from railway
station, last train long departed;
but I'd booked a wake-up call
– and caught the early morning one.

KNOWINGLY

Always ahead of me
in his well-informed refrain,
'Yes, I know,' says he loftily
– then scrabbles on with rope
or net he's mending in the mud
by slidey-bottomed boat
he'd dragged up on the bank;

Why he listens as I talk
I cannot tell, for he senses
simply everything with eye
that discards all but what
he really needs to know;
though I did surprise him once
when I showed him how to row!

FUNNY VALENTINE

You can snicker, you can smile,
you can tease me for a while
but when it's my turn to beguile
you'll be mesmerised by style
– and smile and smile and smile,
for that's the silliness of love.

But if the laughter doesn't last
you'll be sure the love is past
and the consequence is vast
for you might as well recast
your net and look around once more
for another life to share.

WATER

A torrent of rain
after it the heat again,
sandy river

Masaoka Shiki

Sun-soaked soil blisters bright
then crumbles dun as dust
to wait the puddle-thump
of rain that makes a broth,
browning mud to leach
to reaching root of tree,
anointing seed (fresh-born)
to cotyledon green,
wetting too through
pastureland that tilts
towards a gloating sea.

LADY BE BETTER

MOON

A big coin moon shines on me tonight,
the kind that wishes for a face,
smiling at my fecklessness
as I try to find a missing word
to complete this jigsaw life.

Streaming clouds reveal, intermittently,
that cold-rock presence, front lit
by hidden circumnutating sun
on a night I'll never see again
– closeness not for fifty years to come.

The Next Blue Note

TRUMPET SMILE

He played with Buddy Bolden,
even wrote a song to him,
and all of New Orleans
was nothing but a band to him,
but when he lost his teeth
his trumpet wouldn't blow for him
When the Saints Come Marching In;

Bunk Johnson was a name
to conjure with in those
golden days away, and spoke
ensemble-style in recorded
jazz we listen to today –
but because he lost his teeth,
his trumpet wouldn't blow for him;

King Oliver and Johnny Dodds,
young Kid Ory and that Satchmo
were the guys who gigged with him,
and Jimmie Noone and Jelly Roll
and Bechet with his saxophone
were other jazzmen known to him
– until his trumpet wouldn't blow;

The bands played on without him
and Bunk slunk into memory

Lady Be Better

– until they found him cutting
logs down Louisiana way
and had a whip-round for a cornet,
while Bechet's dentist brother Len
made a set of teeth for him;

With white smile back in place again,
he formed an all-star ragtime band
and played his own Bunk's Blues,
belting out I Can't Escape From You
and When I Leave the World Behind
on discs cut sixty years ago
in trumpet tribute to his friends.

The Next Blue Note

TURN AND TURNABOUT

His thoughts are like ripples
on the surface of a chucked-stone pond
– you can see them on his wrinkled brow.
What's he got to worry about?
Hasn't he seen another's death before?
But this is different, circumstance
is just that – his turn has come around.

The hood is pulled down on his head
by someone else who should be dead;
but war's a funny thing, they say.
He keeps on looking in his mind,
sees only that last image of the sky
– and waits for drop and rending tug,
the chance to kick out at the air.

Lady Be Better

JAZZ ME BLUES

The whip-poor-will of clarinet
or pecker tap of roisting drum
and thrum of a double bass
– sound pronounced in piano mode
and rump of trombone pumping slide;

And, cutting through, that piercing
ditty shriek of trumpet thrall
colouring in the notes, abjuring
boundaries of time – magnitude
of sound slashing out a pathway

through the jungle of a life
not yet slowing down a beat;
while she who blues me from afar
(who cast a purple shadow
on my mind) – I hear her call

above the din and scramble on
in fearful search of tattered
memory, certain then that cadence
speaks when harmony turns back
to join the fold in unity.

The Next Blue Note

FAME GAME

Hunched, the writing man; words flow
through his fingers trippingly,
straightened then, bolt upright
in paused thought, pouncing down again
to trap the notion in,
bracketed in parenthetic clause,
long-net rabbiting his field
of pure imagination.

But will it sell, this masterpiece
of hothouse cosseting,
for who wants other people's passion?
Will it make a script for Hollywood?
He cracks a smile and strikes a prose,
purple now – and deepening,
digging for that critical
acclaim so desperately desired.

TIDAL RACE

Wednesday dawn in Widnes,
sliding through the mist:
'Backstops crew,' cries coxen,
'come forward now to row'
– as oars gouge into water,
eight at once in time,
in and out the sequence,
slicing river slime,
bellnotes chiming out the tempo
while canvas cuts a wake;
this is our day to practise,
nine men seated in a boat.

BOG BEGINNINGS

Asphodel in aspic,
bog-dwelling plant of shame,
why do you present
such flashy aspect
in all that stench disdain?

Do you strain to live again
through others' death decay?
Yes, you flush out hope
with spire of gold to light
warmonger nights of gloom.

You pre-ordain a time
for peace when bogland
quakes with yellow spark
– for trepidation never
saved a nation in despair.

Lady Be Better

YOU AGAIN!

I glance at you and cross
that unsafe bridge of thoughts
half-kindled – and a flame
of recognition drags
me to the other side
of memory; but where
have I seen that face before?
Not in my dreams, surely?

Suddenly a tune strikes up
and I'm dancing in the dark
at some long-forgotten
hothouse rave with moonlight
sieving through the foliage,
leopard-spotting scattered
clothes – so casually
abandoned in the trees.

And I well remember then
the music that was playing
– it was Sinatra singing
I've Got You Under My Skin –
and you were blaming me
for missing your last train
and asking when we would
be meeting once again.

OFF-BEAT

My teacher used a knuckle stick
when I practised on piano;
no thumbing of the black notes,
if you please, unless you want
another tap, she'd say to me
while the metronome clacked time.

Scales, arpeggios and chords
were just staccato smacks
and I looked forward to duets
when prod was not in reach
and fingering was all my own
while the metronome clacked time.

Counting beats was difficult
with that interfering sound;
it was the music sheet
and only what was in my head
that led to pleasant cadences
– not the metronome that clacked time.

Now the brash of jazz has taught
me how to listen while others
play that cacophony
of sound barred from me by tutting
rule of thumb – and clacking
metronome of ordered time.

MOVING ON

Prise out the grabbing fish-hook
chance that has me gasping
on the deck of landed love;
throw me back to swim away
from suffocating rules I must obey.

Just as you, so me, staring at the sun;
but only you can see what we've begun
to make of this new direction shared.

I'm just not ready to relinquish
the dark moon's hold on me – so let's sleep
a little longer before commitment
takes us on to desert song of danger.
Leave down rucksacks – better still, empty them.

NO STING IN THE TALE

I close the garden gate
on a swarm of wasps;
they congregate
about my head,
I let them out again
– respectfully.

ABSOLUTELY

Peeks through the sonic frontier
of night, that lightning flash
of thought that carried Einstein
off the beaten track; speaks
of wisdom plucked from endless
time and planted firmly
in the present that is fast
becoming past a future
comprehends: That's Life, Sinatra
sings – his way – and makes it all
so simple to my muddled mind.

The Next Blue Note

CAVE PAINTINGS

Pummelled by explosive probings
of a twice-time enemy,
blitz-hit Britain fought to save
its prized possessions – gold reserves
sent to safety of the Falklands
and galleries of art re-hung
beneath a mountain far away.
'If you're happy and you know it,
clap your hands,' sang a London
in defiance of the bombs
while cavalcades of trucks sneaked

old masters off to caves in Wales.
As war is raging over ground
Hero weeps for her Leander drowned,
courtesy of artist Turner's
scintillating brush – and passing
them in rural river bliss,
a masterpiece by Constable
of cart and horse and wain of hay,
while Saskia as Flora gazes
seductively on Blake's mad King Neb

as he claws his way along the ground.
Outside, Van Dyck's King Charles
trots magnificently

Lady Be Better

along overlooking hill.
Eighteen hundred canvasses
character the slate mine walls
in silent ghostly presences
while Europe wages war –
and head bailiff charged with guarding
them takes to potting at the bats
to break the boredom of his task.

> *In 1940, with Germany's Luftwaffe blitzing Britain, Churchill ordered convoys of vans and lorries – cunningly marked CHOCOLATE – to ferry works of art from London's galleries to the safety of Manod slate quarry caves in Blaenau Ffestiniog, North Wales, for the duration of the war.*

WILDERNESS

Mountain sky's lime green today, Sahara
evening, envying the lush of land
beyond – just the place for forty days
and forty nights of abstinence
watching belly-riding snake curve
across the desiccated rock
in silent quest for blood of sustenance;
a time when fantasies of peace replacing
war and milk and honey, bread and fish
aplenty fill the gasping mind with yearn
for nearly-there beguiling journey's end.

COOL FOR CATS

Four cats she had – Rockall,
Finisterre, Hebrides
and Bailey, well suited
to all weathers – moderate,
poor, becoming good, cyclone
at times, five to seven
later if you please, when hungry
for a bit of German Bight.
They strayed, of course, last seen
in Humber, Thames and Dover.

The Next Blue Note

ON REFLECTION

I have a cupboard full of mirrors
never looked at, hoarded from a past
since locked from sight as is my face
from you – now that you've moved on, switched
horses in mid-song so unexpectedly.

I think now's the time to break that door,
smash the telling glass to smithereens
with sledge of heavy heart and look again
on my reflection – but only in
the stream that flows away from home.

Lady Be Better

HEY-HO!

We buried you by village pond,
just where we'd caught you by the leg;
silver foil for shroud and Goldflake
box your cask – and we said a prayer
and sang a froggie song, 'mibbits'
for the chorus shouted by our gang.
And in the spring the spawn appeared
on flooded bank with yellow packet
floating on the speckled glug.
Hey, there's Anthony, we said.

ALIEN

It came from planet X,
blow-in without a name;
we called it Alien
and taught it how to speak
in words we'd understand;
soon we called it *him* or *you*
and *he* learned from us
of peace and war but favoured
'harmony' – and forever
talked of *we*, but never
once did Alien say *I*.

BURIED TREASURE

My beech tree hanging bank
is spangled now with mushroom
crop this apple-drop time of year
– marking the spot where I buried
the cat and a squirrel
that fell to its accurate paw.

Red fairy agaric
and sulphurous ceps
in jungle-rust caps
make steps that streel upwards
to witch-hatted patterns
with upside-down look

and carbuncles of saffron
to fill out the wedges
of dazzle display – preyed
and preyed-upon prey
now favoured by plants
that suck life from decay.

TEST OF TIME

Earth's camber greets the sky at dawn
with precision ink that marks
the day's parade without nostalgia
for the night-slept past and leaves me
blinking back the tears, remembering
how you are no longer there to share
this life we built together – dreaming
it would never end so suddenly.

Now I live and think of how things
might have been, instead of snapping
slick salute to meet the testing
time to come; but I'll wait on a bit,
while Mahler's scream with trumpet note
hangs my anguish out to dry, dissonance
unresolved until a kinder key brings
calmer mood to sally forth again.

Lady Be Better

AN EVENING WITH COURTNEY PINE

Jazz night has us reaching out and waving,
bumping fists with Courtney Pine, his big fat
yulping sax in revolution mode,
a far-off cry from Way Down Yonder
in New Orleans and Rampart Street Parade
– staccato tongue licking off the quavers
like a Bren on rapid fire, rat-a-tat
crescendoing in breathless bomb-raid
siren wail, triumphal merriment of song
freed from gravitas of earthbound gravity,
streeling black notes oiled with tears of joy
as tunes familiar peel out from long improvs
of sounding pipe, hot toast melodies
dandied up in new identities
to keep the A Train running on its rails;
old ones, new ones, borrowed ones, blue
ones – no mood escapes the magic reedman's
Ali Baba thievings once the genie's out.

The Next Blue Note

ILL MET BY SUNLIGHT

A plane lampoons the freshly-painted
landscape, leaving torn-cloud contrail
and turbo-jet excrescences – graffiti
scrawl across millennia of time.
She looks at me, expectantly, and speaks.

I cannot hear her voice above the jet's
ripped-curtain noise; a lapwing lollops through
the foreground sky as she talks on, questioning:
'Haven't we met somewhere?' (Screwing up her eyes
against the sun.) Now this is *my* chat-up

line – it's never been this way before.
A compliment should follow. 'I'd know that face
anywhere. You look fed-up, lonely.'
Not quite my style but not bad either.
Some interest, some concern. Me? My way

is one part kindness, two parts lust. 'I walk
this way with my dog each day. I've not seen
you here before.' The plane has vanished,
we're now alone with only earthbound sound
of our own voices. But I haven't

spoken yet – which is unusual for me.
She goes on: 'I like the solitude

Lady Be Better

and now you've broken it, you're trespassing
– but that's all right. I *do* know you, I saw
you on stage once.' She's going to ask me

for my autograph. That will be a first!
I fumble for my pen. 'You weren't very
good. You must have been having an off night.'
The dog pulls at the lead and she walks on.
Never mind the jet – I am *her* graffiti.

The Next Blue Note

LADY BE BETTER

It is the primacy of pulsing beat
that draws me to the Basie band,
how saxman Lester Young's dry harmony
stands alone against the tidal wave
of riffs in unison laid down
by well-honed brass: Lady Be Good
could not be better in their hands,
nor of their successors playing today.
But as for me, I sometimes think I am
that guy the song's about, alone once more,
misunderstood; Oh, Lady Be Good
again to me and we can spin that tune
with Lester serenading us on sax!

NUTS!

Pops a cachou,
cups her hand
to check her breath,
nods in affirmation
of her sweetness;

But he could have
told her that –
he chews and sucks
on every thought of her;
she's his favourite nut!

BY THE SEASIDE

Bill Vernon was a force for fun
with boxer's fists and red silk
linings to his slickly-tailored suits
and wives and mistresses to match
– proud to come from Morecambe
with his shiny seaside face.

He settled down in Clacton
and owned a small hotel,
catering for charabancs
of people from up North;
much drink was had by all
and small-time bow-tie gangsters
played the fruit machine
while Ken the Caterpillar
had them sing in harmony:

Beautiful dreamer,
wake unto me,
starlight and dewdrops
are waiting for thee.

It was bingo for the elderly
and Palm Court orchestras
along the gull-white front
and Redcoats at the Butlins

Lady Be Better

Camp and jellied eels on sale
– and Ted Heath blasting out
his big-band repertoire
on wave-lashed wooden pier.

Ken Higgins, musician and member of the Caterpillar Club – last rear-gunner of a Lancaster to parachute out and live. RIP.

SLICE OF LIFE

Fetch down the mattock now,
slice through the roots of gorse
knowing bush will grow again,
yellow bloom bursting into song
like a church choir practising.

Undergrowth is there to keep
us constantly provoked:
tidy minds need exercise
as thoughts grow scattier
with time and seek direction.

Lady Be Better

WEATHER WARNING

Nicely runs the river
down the hill,
quietly sounds the water
over rock,
warmly shines the sun
on single sessile oak;

But you should have seen it
when the flash-floods came:
torrents tearing
overcoated mountain
into rags
and beating down the trees

with mud and boulder
Armageddon slide!
No, do not be tricked
by life's tranquillity:
seek shelter
when weather says you can.

PASSING

*How much longer
is my life?
A brief night...*

Masaoka Shiki

His dry laugh ticks in tribute
to death's mud song – and he is gone,
a blade that cut with rough-edged
sword a swathe through life he owned.

Remember days that lasted
way beyond the shine of sun?
And night-time lit by jinx as high
as merriment could guy?

Leavings of the much-loved man
are not wasted on lives of fun
– devilish doings of children's
sons and daughters yet to come.

ALLEGHENY MAN

Allegheny Man

MOUNTAIN GREENERY

Chasing mountain peak, I cross the path
of bladder fern and rock stonecrop,
then saxifrage and fir clubmoss
bring me on to base of scree, butter-pat
lines of long-healed scars, so swiftly drawn
by artist's pen, scrubbed now by light
of effervescent early morning sun;
then on and up the higher hang,
back-and-footing through a broken crack
that widens to an easy chimney stack;
mantel-shelfing now to ledge eyed from below –
and finding there, lurking luscious in the shade,
a precious little Snowdon lily flower
with leaves a sheen of green so rarely seen
at altitude – not even in a dream.

The Next Blue Note

ON STATE STREET

Bejesus-bearded,
unmiraculously dressed,
he played his saxophone
– tapping out of time
with lives of passers-by
who couldn't give a toss.

And you should've heard him rant!
Between the tipple and the sax
he dealt a ditch of words
for anyone who'd listen,
claiming he'd hit the bottom
dollar – times were hard as dimes.

But pride had never left his eyes
which sparkled blue as sky,
while rain began to fill
his wishing well – making
islands of the coins
so grudgingly thrown in.

With heart he played – and not
a little soul, and when he reached
crescendo of the set
with Royal Garden Blues,
pedestrians were forced
to stop and turn and chuck

Allegheny Man

their paper money in;
then his grin was like the sun
had come to shine on him
– he'd buy himself another
lushy glug and give them
Tishomingo Rag again.

The Next Blue Note

GO WITH THE FLOW

Come, lean with me across this bridge,
see the river run from left to right
– weed flexing in the flow, just hanging on;
hear the music of the water, tuned
by pebble-shift and slanting of a rock,
and know, no doubt, that frequency will shape
with flood or drought as brightness, whiteness
interchange with shadows cast by sun;
hope for glimpse of fish, speckled grace of trout
finning in and out of places hidden
from the light; dream your thoughts away
downstream, knowing they will never come
to you again on this ancient arch of stone.

Allegheny Man

I HAD A DREAM

– after visiting Virginia

Do you ever get a feeling
that a place, a people past,
peels off on you? I do.

Sometimes it's as if
I get sucked in by the essence
of awareness and carry it
away with me when I move on.

Do birds and animals feel this?
Are we gifted with some long-lost
state of mind they share?

Is that why we dream
exotically? Or am I speaking
mumbo-jumbo – gushing poetry
like some charlatan?

My gran would have had
a word for it. It is 'the jizz',
she'd say, peering at the leaves.

Do we have faith? A resounding
no, I think. Pragmatically,
it's guff – welling up the Welsh
in me. But all the same …

The Next Blue Note

ALLEGHENY MAN

I knocked and heard a screech and razzle-clump
across a wooden floor – and then I saw
him in the open door, half-in, half-out,
sitting in a chair he'd built to spare
his wooden leg while waiting for repair.
Bartle John his name, though no one knew
from whence he came, a mountain man for sure,
with bear to blame for brutal loss of limb;
whiz mechanic, so they said, who walked

with miracles he worked on bits
of old machinery – and strummed the blues on banjo
made from shagbark hickory, with God-knows-what
for strings, and twanged his 'itty-bitty
trickiness', sometimes 'til moon had bled
into the sun and Allegheny hills
had begun to run with colour of the day.
Now he's gone, panning for the stars – but still
they hear his music drifting in the wind

as curled leaves settle on his grotesque
rotting chair, while salamanders crawl
across the hanging door and tawny
crescent butterflies flutter through the roof.
They say old Bartle John sure could play
and sing the saddest song about life's

Allegheny Man

wrongs he saw so clearly through unmatched
eyes of blue and brown which understood
alternate sides of neighbours' arguments.

We never really met – yet in the ruins
of his home, I feel I know him well;
his heavy presence lingers there
like a pulsing shimmer in the air,
while mockingbird and phoebe
stay their song – creatures dumb in awe
of spirit lore, listening for that moving
chair to squeal across the hallowed ground
where Allegheny Man once ruled with sound.

The Next Blue Note

NIGHT LIFE

The nightjar swoops and yaws
and churrs its song, cracks
its white-blobbed wings
in little echoes off the *clog*
that rears from moorland heath;

Dusk has come and insects
rising from the sun-warmed
ground are targeted
relentlessly in waddle
airborne frenzy feed;

Attracted by its signal
flight, a drabber, mottled
mate with bristle gape
joins the 'jar in Morfa
Bychan's fading light;

Below, an adder winds
between the bracken stems
in secret stalk of pulsing
prey that will not live
to see another day;

While, steep above them all,
a kestrel hovers

Allegheny Man

with the same intent;
higher still, a silver streak
tears a crevice in the sky;

Night descends on land
once occupied by sea –
and mountains to the north
and east of Wales
vanish in the purple gloom.

The Next Blue Note

SHAKE AND RATTLE

I have a piece of hollow quartz
with stone that rattles from inside.
It's sometimes said a core of gold
is hidden in such rock; mine's from
Gwynfynydd's long-gone worked-out dig.

I like to shake it and imagine
glow of wealth I do not have,
but I'll never break it open
to find out: it wouldn't, couldn't
beat its music for me then.

I feel the same reluctance
with a conch from which I hear
the sigh of sea shut in a shell
cast up by raging waves
half a world away from me.

Gwynfynydd gold mine, near Dolgellau, North Wales.

CROSSED LINES

When you rang me,
what I said to you
was what I meant
to say to her.

If I give you her
number, you can
call and pass
the message on.

This is the second
time I've telephoned
to tell you this.
Hello? Are you still there ... ?

LIKE FATHER, LIKE SON

It had to be me –
over the top first.
The wasps were in the tree;
take the banger, they'd said,
light it, let it flare
and drop it in the nest
– piece of cake for you.

Brock' s Blockbuster,
the firework label said,
biggest whizz of all –
better than a Standard
Thunder Flash, or Pains
or Wells, the other
brands we brats knew.

Outriders stung me twice
before I'd lobbed it in
and then I had to jump
down from the branch
to land on leafy bank
– but my satchel strap
left me dangling.

The blast took out the bark
and the swarm surrounded me,

Allegheny Man

then headed for my friends
as if they were to blame;
I was left unscathed
'til father rescued me
and men cut down the tree.

Years on I taught my son
to climb and we dangled
upside down like trapeze men;
now his son does just the same
– but since he's only six
I stand below to catch him
if the branch should break.

The Next Blue Note

WHAT TO DO

Holding court astride the days
that go so unremarked,
I bless my luck in health restored
and resolve to cram them
with experience – but what to do?
The questions keep on coming.

Invent something? Re-train
as an astronaut? Get out
more? Buy another stick insect?
Become a poet, even?
No, I think I'll just wait and see
what happens next to me.

Allegheny Man

LEAN OF LIFE

With bent branch trimmed
to take the weight
of crooked lean
he slashed at lick
of leaf, knowing
hook would undercut
the hurt of stooping
back to come.

Seeing me watching
him, he thrust the stick
in my direction
as if to say,
One day you'll
be as me;
I nodded then,
painfully.

AGAIN

Spring has broken through and sprung,
liberating beds of truculence
– wishing winter washed away
and greening mud replacing
white cold-binding snow;
a trembling chaffinch pair spin
round and round in mating dash
and chase across pulsating ground;
and eyeing all this display,
the swagger fox in russet
splendour, strolling in the sun
with all good time to spare
– and his hunger yet to come.

Allegheny Man

CONDITION RED

Oh, my passive pluperfect
love, you who've been had
by me and me by you
in passion without end,
will we ever make
a future free of tense?

What is your condition?
Mine is Red. I'm no King
Kong on Empire State
with nowhere else to go
– but thoughts of you
make me want to conjugate.

ALL DRESSED IN BLACK

Tidy settlements of summer hay,
Weetabixed and wrapped in hijab black,
ordained for winter fodder feed
– so neat the countryside
as man proclaims control, ruling
nature from the cabin of a tractor.

But look, the matching-coloured crows
have come to sift the seed between the bales
– and joining them, a lazy lilt
of lapwings with stand-up crests waving
in the breeze, pee-wit-calling as they land;
a pheasant lends its colour to the scene.

Allegheny Man

HORSES FOR COURSES

I think I passed
your Rorschach test:
I re-hung your daubs
the other way
and understood
their meaning;
but you, the artist,
couldn't see
it as I did.

The Next Blue Note

GOOD MORNING BLUES

Shape-shifting thoughts spread disharmony:
droplets of mercury in crucible
of deadliness, stone eagles defying
gravity in flight; those waking dreams
come phlegming up again; outside I know
the sun is beating at the gate, inside
all is night; but dark times cannot last
for long – so I'll pretend to pop
a pill and wait 'til black-dog bark is gone.

Allegheny Man

PITY THE WIND

The wind's a terrorist today,
blowing up the hemisphere
– barbarian laying waste
with indiscriminate intent.

It's tearing branches from the trees,
amputees without the chance
of normal numbing autumn fall,
and furrowing the seas to seed

the growth of pulverising
tidal power in seismic
consequence for undefended
shrinking lands of gentleness.

Yet, without this diabolic
pressure change, a zephyr calm
can soothe-caress a land and sea
with supplicant apology,

and only devastation left
for all to see reminds us
of that ever-present jeopardy,
for nothing ever stays the same.

The Next Blue Note

HOLEY MOLEY!

Slasher. He's the man
who's got designs
on you – puts the holes
in fashion clothes;
conspicuously poor,
that's what people
pay to be.
Ripped jeans? No bother,
do it quicker
than a moth.
Next year we'll all
be naturists.

Allegheny Man

THE HARE THAT DIPPED ITS PAWS

The hare that dipped its paws
was on the beach each day,
bathing in the suck-back
trickle of the waves.

It might have been a child
at paddle-play and seemed
to love the sun that dried
its prints into the sand.

Joining it one time
were its leverets
– offspring out to share
the healing seaside fun.

Last day I visited
the shore, the young
were there alone – searching
through the gentle waves.

TIME CHANGE

'I wasted time and now doth time waste me.'[2]

No, I'll wait for the next blue note,
then we'll do our time together.
Four-four's the bluest beat to go
– life's to be enjoyed, isn't it?

Iambic pentameter's no great Shakes.

---

[2] *Richard II*

Allegheny Man

SEEING IS BELIEVING

On a picnic summer's day
with shimmer in the air,
my second-sighted gran
spotted Romans leading mules
half-hidden by the hanging mist
in silent stumble over rocks
that marked Llanbedr Steps;

'Look, they carry copper
from the mines,' she excited
said to me – but I saw
only sandwich, cake and bun
and tipped away the tealeaves
lest she tell me more to come
in a life so recently begun.

The Next Blue Note

INSIDE OUT

I have a bottle in a ship;
it leans along the mantel shelf,
just where it always did, nuzzling
soft in its vintage years of dust;
it was my uncle's little joke
to construct a sloop around
his favoured plonk – a Fleurie
'fifty-nine, long drunk, just like
he must have been the day he laid
it down, neck thrusting from the bow,
cork-carved figurehead made
to look like Marilyn Monroe.

BLUEING THE BLUES

Blue is the note I blow
for you in jazz-felt harmony;
red is my desire for you
until the black when you've moved on;
green is the sad-felt jealousy
when I imagine where you've gone;
blue is back again when mood
replays those memories
in sounds which help me cope alone.

MOMENTS

Loafing languid in the sun,
watching puff clouds buff the sky;

Your broken nail, cerise on sheet,
lacquered scratch of reckless love;

Plop of fish I didn't see,
rippling round mysteriously;

You, sealing passion into paint
with supple twist of wrist;

Curfew call of curlew
closing down the day;

First time meeting you, eye-to-eye
in shared incredulity;

I could go on – but moments'
meanings shuffled off with you.

Allegheny Man

CARD-BORED

I remember often
seeing my bored and lonely
'housewife' mum crouching
on the carpet floor,
stacking kings and queens
and jacks in solitary

patience game – her
frustrated intellect
jokered into decks
of calming pliancy
while she waited
'his' return from work.

That carpet too held
the secret of her tears,
for I'd sometimes woken
in the night to hear her
crying – and tried, as child,
to halve her sorrow.

The Next Blue Note

SOUNDS FAMILIAR

Sometimes I hear the waterfall
when wind is blowing right,
sound winging in my window
on a summer's night;
other days, a sea mist
from another compass
point brings salty smells
to me – better than the slurry
stink from rain-wet field above.

On drowsy afternoons when sun
is high, the hum of insects
fills the sky with chorus
of the bumblebee and midge
and ordinary fly.
At night, a bark of vixen
fox or squeal of rabbit caught
will bring mortality to mind;
Blues Jumped the Rabbit was the song

of this, I think – and once, only
once, in twenty years, a cuckoo
came and called and I remembered
Beethoven's clever clarinet
in his Pastoral Symphony.
I watched it sounding on the ash

Allegheny Man

until it flew on south;
I wish it would return to me,
bringing fluted nightingale!

Now, with distant regularity,
a big plane passes overhead
bound for Montreal where we met
by chance and I told you all of this:
my stone-built cottage home and birds
and bees and sounds and smells,
log fires and winter howl of wind
– but you only spoke to me
in words of French, *tant pis*.

TROUBLE AHEAD?

Take you and me and juxtapose:
suppose that I were you instead
– would I then hate myself
for what you saw in me?
And would your newly-found
disdain balance things again?
Let's make another start and see.

SWIMMING WITH A MANATEE

Ugliness is relative,
it seems to me
after swimming
with a manatee.
Its pale eye under water
seemed repulsed by me
– or was it just
my blue wetsuit
that displeased?
The feeling's mutual.

DEEP BLUE SEA

In my wildest dream
I had this image
once – of trombone
poking from the sea
and sliding at the sun
in deepest harmony
with breakers romping
at the shore, splashing
sax and double bass
– and Armstrong standing
there, trumpet dangled
at his side, dabbing
at perspiring face
with pressed white handkerchief
from pile on shiny black
piano top, sighing,
'Oooh yeaah …'

SORREL

Where a hill slope,
a snug of trees, where trees,
a small flower grows

Masaoka Shiki

Escaping rasping slough of autumn chill,
in moss deep-over, wood sorrel vaunts
its petal droop of pink-on-white,
dynamite of colour unsparked
by spring in copse full-skirting fall of hill;
now, fattening dew drops roll down the stem
of solitary plant, nourishing roots
at hem: a life begins, just here, again.

www.ingramcontent.com/pod-product-compliance
Lightning Source LLC
Chambersburg PA
CBHW022119040426
42450CB00006B/767